# THE 7 CHARACTER STRENGTHS OF HIGHLY SUCCESSFUL STUDENTS™

# SELF- CONTROL

RAMONA SIDDOWAY

rosen publishing's
rosen
central®

NEW YORK

Published in 2014 by The Rosen Publishing Group, Inc.
29 East 21st Street, New York, NY 10010

First Edition

**Library of Congress Cataloging-in-Publication Data**

Siddoway, Ramona.
Self-control/Ramona Siddoway.—First edition.
    pages cm.—(The 7 character strengths of highly successful students)
Includes bibliographical references and index.
ISBN 978-1-4488-9543-4 (library binding)—ISBN 978-1-4488-9563-2 (pbk.)—
ISBN 978-1-4488-9564-9 (6-pack)
1. Self-control in children—Juvenile literature. 2. Self-control in adolescence—
Juvenile literature. 3. Self-control—Juvenile literature. I. Title.
BF723.S25S53 2014
179'.9—dc23

                                                                    2013000709

*Manufactured in the United States of America*

CPSIA Compliance Information: Batch #S13YA: For further information, contact Rosen Publishing, New York, New York, at 1-800-237-9932.

# CONTENT

INTRODUCTION 4

## CHAPTER 1
THE POWER OF
SELF-CONTROL 7

## CHAPTER 2
EMOTIONAL SELF-CONTROL 15

## CHAPTER 3
ACADEMIC SELF-CONTROL 24

## CHAPTER 4
PHYSICAL SELF-CONTROL 34

## CHAPTER 5
ACHIEVING SELF-CONTROL 42

GLOSSARY 50

FOR MORE INFORMATION 52

FOR FURTHER READING 56

BIBLIOGRAPHY 58

INDEX 62

# INTRODUCTION

**M**any people don't realize that self-control involves courage. Self-control is making ourselves do things that we don't want to do in order to achieve a goal, especially when there may be a lot of exciting temptations and distractions around us. It's about managing emotions and thoughts and controlling one's behavior. It means giving up something good now in order to obtain and enjoy something better later.

Self-control can involve any activity or pursuit that a person wants to do better or an area in which he or she wants to improve. The goal might be to stop procrastinating or biting one's nails, staying on a diet, controlling a temper, or just sticking with a resolution.

Gabby Douglas is a typical sixteen-year-old who loves hanging out with friends, shopping, and eating junk food when she can. But in order to take home two gold medals from the 2012 Summer Olympics in gymnastics, Gabby had to carefully regulate all of the leisure activities in her life. She had to prioritize work

U.S. gymnast Gabby Douglas poses on the podium with her gold medal during the London 2012 Olympic Games. It was at this moment that she knew that all the self-control she had developed was worth it.

over pleasure and free time to be able to practice long hours and fully prepare for the Olympic Games.

While many think of persistence when they think of Gabby Douglas, it also took a lot of self-control for this teenager to get to the Olympics.

Gabby didn't watch television, go to the mall or movies with friends, or even just hang out with her family. Instead, she chose to put in long hours at the gym in order to become the first African American to win the gold medal in the women's individual all-around competition. She lived and trained 2,000 miles (3,219 kilometers) from home. Gabby was so homesick and tired that, just six months before the Olympic Games, she wanted to quit and go home. It took a lot of self-control to set aside the temptation to give up, go home, and stop training. But when she was standing on the podium in London, she realized, "This was worth it!"

Think about what could be achieved with more self-control in life: better grades, better self-esteem, less depression, and better management of anger issues. With more self-control, a person is better able to keep promises, be more reliable, and get along better with people both at school and at home.

Don't worry if you feel like you don't have much self-control right now. Very few people are born with this character strength. It may take some effort, willful choice, self-awareness, and commitment. But self-control can be learned, practiced, and internalized. Like any other kind of strength you develop, the character strength of self-control requires practice, repetition, and lots of effort. The payoff—success in almost every imaginable endeavor, from friendships and schoolwork to romantic relationships and career building—makes it all worthwhile and lasts your entire lifetime.

## CHAPTER 1

# THE POWER OF SELF-CONTROL

Researchers at Duke University in Durham, North Carolina, and King's College in London, England, studied one thousand people from New Zealand. They tracked them from birth to age thirty-two. They found that of these one thousand people, those who struggled with self-control as preschoolers were three times more likely to have poor physical health, substance abuse problems, financial problems, and criminal records as adults.

Several years ago a man named Walter Mischel conducted another famous experiment on self-control. He put four-year-olds in a room by themselves with one marshmallow each. Mischel told each child that he or she could eat the marshmallow immediately, or, if the child waited until he came back to the room, he or she would get two marshmallows. Of the 653 kids in the study, two-thirds gave in to temptation and ate the single marshmallow.

As in the later study of New Zealanders, Mischel followed his test subjects for years and discovered that those children who exercised self-control in the marshmallow experiment went on to much more successful adult lives.

## WHAT IS SELF-CONTROL?

Self-control is more than just waiting to obtain or experience something better later on. It is taking charge of what we say, do, and even think. It takes discipline to change negative or self-defeating thoughts into positive ideas. Self-control is

Staying focused on work assignments requires self-control. The effort will pay off in higher grades and achievement and expanded life opportunities.

doing what is right when you are supposed to and avoiding doing things that are wrong. Some examples of situations that may require self-control are:

- Staying focused on schoolwork
- Cleaning your room (instead of watching television or giving in to other distractions)
- Telling the truth
- Not lashing out when someone has hurt you
- Raising your hand and waiting to speak
- Controlling your temper
- Avoiding peer pressure
- Avoiding harmful substances, like drugs and alcohol
- Saying appropriate things and resisting the urge to say inappropriate things

## BORN THIS WAY?

There is a difference between character strength and talent or ability. A person may not be born with the coordination and grace of Gabby Douglas, but everyone can learn the same self-mastery she has displayed throughout her gymnastics career. We are all born with innate talents and gifts. But it takes willpower and mindfulness to turn those gifts into usable traits.

How can you tell if you are getting better at self-control? When you begin developing self-control skills, you will start to feel a sense of ownership of yourself and your life.

This means that you will feel like this is the real you, that you have a better sense of control over your actions, reactions, thoughts, and behavior. When self-control skills become

# A SELF-CONTROL QUIZ

## ASK YOURSELF THESE QUESTIONS:

1. When I make up an exercise schedule, can I stick to it?
2. Do I resist the urge to go to the movies when I need to stay home and study?
3. Do I often lose my temper and say harsh things to friends, family, classmates, and teachers that I later regret?
4. Do I often get into physical confrontations with people?
5. Do I occasionally abuse alcohol or drugs?
6. Do I procrastinate a lot and find myself rushing to complete an assignment at the last minute that I had weeks to work on?
7. Do I overreact to stressful or emotional situations?
8. Do I often make the choice that is easiest and offers short-term pleasure or avoidance of work and effort?
9. Do I have trouble making and keeping friends?
10. Do I often get into trouble for impulsive words or actions?

If you answered "yes" to three or more of these questions, you may currently have a lack of self-control. With some dedicated practice and effort, however, you can gain mastery over both yourself and your life.

stronger, it is possible to move more easily and successfully through every aspect of life. This includes your home life, school life, work life, and social life. There will be less fear of losing self-control in the future.

## I OWN THIS!

There will probably be a sense of excitement when a person first starts to use and practice self-control. The more self-control is practiced in one area, the more motivation there will be to use it in other areas of life.

Choosing to buckle down and finish chores rather than procrastinating will enable a person to be successful in other areas involving self-control. It also boosts one's pride and self-esteem.

And with each success—whether it be through exercising self-control by choosing to study, deciding to pay attention to a lecture, choosing not to lash out at members of an opposing sports team, or realizing it is better to buckle down and finish chores rather than making a fuss or procrastinating—that person will have a greater sense of pride and self-esteem.

When learning how to regulate emotions, thoughts, and behavior, a person becomes empowered to pursue any goal that is important to him or her. He or she will have a greater chance of going to college, finding a good job, getting married, and having a family. And not only will that person achieve these goals, he or she will also likely experience great success in all of these fields of endeavor. Self-control is like a muscle: the more it is used, the stronger it becomes.

## BOUNDARIES

Everyone has boundaries, even adults. Boundaries are not handcuffs limiting our freedom. Rather, they enhance and expand our freedom. Think of a kite. It's the string you hold onto that enables a kite to fly high and for long periods of time. Cut the string and the kite drifts beyond your control or crashes to the ground. Boundaries and self-control are like that string on a kite. They guide and direct our lives so that we have more freedom, not less. It's best to get accustomed to boundaries and practicing self-control. As an adult, there will be many times in which it will be required.

**Practice redirecting thoughts rather than allowing them to follow negative pathways. The brain will attempt to turn positive thoughts into reality.**

Part of the secret of demonstrating self-control is in redirecting thoughts in a particular direction rather than allowing them to wander aimlessly or habitually go down negative pathways. Our brains try to make our thoughts real. So if the thoughts are centered on the positive—an "I can do this" attitude—then the brain will do its best to make that thought become a reality. It will find a way to validate and facilitate that message.

Emotions are another key component of the self-control process. Trying to "change" your feelings or pretend that they don't exist may not always be feasible. Try to keep emotions within workable bounds, but don't deny or ignore them. When strong emotions surface, practice addressing them in a calm, responsible, and healthy manner. Just remember that specific emotions don't last forever. With consistent practice, it is easier to move toward a more positive emotional state. Redirecting negative thoughts can help you manage emotions in appropriate ways.

# CHAPTER 2

# EMOTIONAL SELF-CONTROL

At the age of seventeen, Michaela DePrince is a professional ballerina. Getting to where she is now required work, faith, and courage. It also involved a conscious decision to turn away from the horrors of her past as a war orphan in Sierra Leone.

Before being adopted by an American family at the age of four, Michaela witnessed her father's murder by rebels, the starvation of her mother, and the murder of a pregnant caretaker at the orphanage where she lived. Life at this orphanage was very difficult. The caretakers would number the children according to adoption desirability—the most favored to the least. Michaela was number twenty-seven out of twenty-seven children, the least desirable. As such, she was always the last to get food, toys, assistance, and nurturing.

Michaela said that she chose to cope with these grim experiences and circumstances by focusing on the positive rather than on the negative.

Rather than obsessing over negative things in her past as a war orphan, ballerina Michaela DePrince chooses to focus on positive things, including her bright future as a dancer.

She did not obsess about the horrible things that had been said and done to her and that she had witnessed. Michaela refused to wallow in self-pity or lash out at others. She instead chose to redirect her energy and focus on her future as a dancer.

## THE BENEFITS OF SELF-CONTROL

There are a lot of benefits to displaying emotional self-control. Along with fewer personal problems like obsessive-compulsive patterns, depression, and anxiety, a person with emotional self-control will have much higher levels of self-esteem and self-acceptance.

In addition to personal advantages, there are many social benefits to having emotional self-control. People who consistently demonstrate self-control get along with other people better and are more popular with their peers, both at school and in the workplace. Being in control

People who consistently demonstrate emotional self-control get along better with peers and have more satisfying relationships.

of oneself makes it easier to accommodate and adjust one's behavior in the company of another person. This is especially true if that person is "challenging" or "difficult." Self-control allows for more satisfying relationships and can help you adjust to and work constructively with many differing personalities. A person with self-control is a much better leader and is considered trustworthy, reliable, consistent, and fair.

# THE COMPONENTS OF SELF-CONTROL

There are two important components to the development of self-control. The first is thinking deliberately about our words and actions and making a careful decision about whether or not they are advisable. The second is the exercise of restraint—over emotions, impulses, desires, statements, and actions. First is the thought, then the action. If thoughts can be controlled in the beginning, it makes it easier to control the action that follows.

People who demonstrate self-control get along much better with their families. There is much less conflict, better cohesion, and a greater display of empathy. It is easier to trust and build enduring bonds with someone who won't have a sudden outburst of anger or hostility. Relationships are easier with someone whose emotions—both positive and negative—are not volatile and unpredictable. The self-controlled person will enjoy greater freedom, opportunities, and emotional and even material rewards.

## USE YOUR BRAIN!

For emotional self-control, it is important to identify feelings so that they can be dealt with effectively. Emotions, especially strong, potentially overpowering ones, are said to be "triggered." A trigger is anything—a word or action or thought—that causes an angry or other strong emotional response. Some typical triggers include the following:

**1) Auto-appraiser**—This is the "fight or flight" trigger. It is wired into our brains, and we can't do very much about that. It takes over in an emergency or a situation that requires immediate action. If there is a car coming straight at you, your auto-appraiser takes over to make an immediate decision on how to avoid danger and save your life.

**2) Reflective appraiser**—This trigger occurs if a disappointment or setback is experienced, and the mind starts spiraling downward.

Thoughts often trigger emotions. Recognize that a setback in the present doesn't mean failure for the future. Try to avoid spiraling downward after a disappointment.

Say you fail an exam. It's the thought process that follows that will trigger the emotion. A negative spiral will cause you to think, "Now I won't pass the course. Then I won't finish school. Then I won't get a job. Then my whole future is entirely messed up." The best way to combat this negative spiral is to think about something entirely different. Or you can simply recognize that you might be spiraling downward, far beyond the limited impact of the actual disappointment or setback. Bring the thought process back to the present moment: "OK, so I failed THIS exam. I will try harder and do better on the NEXT exam."

**3) Memory recall**—This is remembering an event and the emotion associated with it. Just as with the reflective appraiser, try thinking about something else or try to associate another, more positive emotion with that same memory. Just by rerouting your thinking process to focus on more positive memories, you can successfully reroute your emotions in the process. This creates a more positive emotional environment for yourself and for those around you. Try to live in the present moment rather than be continually haunted by the past.

**4) Imagination**—This is when you are not accurately remembering the event as it really occurred. Instead, you are putting an unjustifiably negative cast on the events of the past. Try using positive imagination to override and correct this inaccuracy and distortion of memory. Again, try to live in the present moment, not the past.

**5) Discussion**—This trigger involves the company we keep. Often discussions with other people bring up various emotions. To maintain positive and self-regulated emotions, surround yourself with friends, family members, and acquaintances who will be a positive influence in your life and help to build you up, not tear you down.

# ANGER MANAGEMENT

What is anger? It is an emotional and entirely natural response to a threat. Anger is also a secondary emotion. That means a person will always—even if for just a split second—feel another emotion first before feeling anger. That emotion might be fear or pain. It might be a feeling of being trapped, pressured, disrespected, offended, startled, or attacked. Everyone experiences anger, and it's not always a bad thing. Expressing anger in emotionally healthy and appropriate ways is acceptable and often therapeutic.

When you are angry, you might feel your heart racing or an adrenaline surge. This is normal. But if a person is constantly exposed to these physiological changes, various health problems can arise, such as depression, headaches, insomnia, or even more serious diseases.

Signs that someone has an anger problem may include substance abuse, a drop in grades, an uncontrollable temper, physical cruelty to people or animals, and frequently hitting or kicking things when angry or frustrated.

These responses to anger are not acceptable. A person shouldn't stifle or repress his or her anger. But he or she should acknowledge, express, and release it in socially acceptable, nondestructive ways. It is important to learn how to manage anger and conflict. Throughout one's life, challenging situations will be continuously experienced at school, home, the workplace, and within the community.

One good method for expressing anger appropriately is the C.A.G.E method:

- **C—Calm.** Recognize that you need to calm down. Take a deep breath (three if necessary) and count to ten. Try redirecting your mind to more peaceful thoughts, use self-talk, and reassure yourself. It is important to calm down before reacting to a situation.
- **A—Assess.** What was the trigger to your anger? A word? A memory? Determine what the trigger was and acknowledge it. Remember that thoughts are just thoughts. They are not necessarily true or accurate, nor do they represent situations that can't be changed for the better.

- **G—Gauge.** Analyze your choice of available actions/reactions and the consequences attached to each. Have a plan and recognize whether a given course of action will resolve anything or make things worse.
- **E—Empowerment.** Recognize that you control not only the outcome of the situation but also your behavior and your life. You have the right to express your feelings with words. And it is OK to walk away from a person or situation if you feel there is nothing positive to be gained by further interaction or involvement. Just remember: you are in charge of you.

# CHAPTER 3

# ACADEMIC SELF-CONTROL

Januario Lumbo grew up in the aftermath of Angola's civil war. Many of the few "free" public schools were not in fact free. The administration would request "donations" in order to get a particular student bumped to the head of the enrollment waiting list. Januario was finally admitted to the Agostinho Neto High School. There, he began taking classes to not only get a high school diploma, but also to earn a secondary degree in English as a second language (ESL) instruction.

Januario was like most of the other students, except in one important way. He refused to give his teachers bribes in order to pass from one grade to the next. As a result, despite excellent grades, he was twenty-one before he finally finished high school. Despite a national culture that encouraged bribery and corruption, Januario resisted the external pressure and internal temptation to pay to advance to the next level. Even in the subjects in which he struggled,

Januario Lumbo sought to learn and succeed in a classroom environment very much like this one in war-torn Angola. Despite a culture that often encouraged bribery and corruption, some students like Januario opted instead for self-regulation, including extra study time, to pass exams.

Januario maintained his self-control. He took the extra time to learn the subjects the right way—through extra study and assistance from others. He often opted for extra studying over hanging out with friends.

Because of this self-regulation, Januario was well known among his peers and by adults as a young man who was trustworthy, dependable, and honest. He was called upon to lead many school and community projects and teams.

He was known as a young man with a great deal of self-discipline. Currently, Januario is a student at a university in Moscow, Russia. He uses much of his spare time learning Russian in order to better understand his professors and their lectures. But he is successfully passing each class in which he is enrolled.

## GRADES AND IQ

Angela Duckworth understands the importance of self-control as a character trait. She is an assistant professor of psychology at the University of Pennsylvania and is one of the leading researchers in the study of self-control. She found that the ability to delay gratification—no matter how small the desired reward—was a better predictor of academic performance than even intelligence.

"Highly self-disciplined adolescents outperformed their more impulsive peers on every academic-performance variable, including report-card grades, standardized achievement test scores, admission to a competitive high school, and attendance, according to Duckworth." "Intelligence is really important," she continues, "but it's still not as important as self-control." In other words, she found that a teenager with self-control did better academically than a teenager who had a high IQ.

So how do we use self-control to perform better in school? How can we improve our grades even if we are not as smart as the kid sitting next to us in algebra? Self-control in academics involves taking the time to consider the consequences of "now" decisions—like the choice between watching television or studying. It also requires thinking about how these decisions will affect a "later" result like performance on a test, research paper, or class project. In order to achieve one's goals, it is important that a person carefully consider the consequences of actions both taken and not taken.

## MAKING SMART CHOICES

A student does not have to be a genius or "gifted and talented" to make smart academic choices. The following list includes just some of the ways self-control can be practiced and employed in school:

- Listen to and follow directions from a teacher or team leader.
- Raise your hand to answer questions—avoid just blurting out the answer.
- Read directions carefully before rushing into the work.
- Focus on working carefully and diligently rather than finishing quickly.

Exercising self-control by being in school every day and on time and focusing on what a teacher is saying will ensure greater academic success.

- Reject shortcuts that will result in you turning in a sloppy or incomplete assignment.
- Meet all of your deadlines, well in advance if possible.
- Be a full participant in group projects; do not let others do your share of the work.
- Focus on the teacher or assignment; avoid distractions.
- Be in school every day and on time. Missing school makes it harder to keep up with assignments and important lectures.
- Part of successful self-regulation involves organization. Many students waste a lot of time just trying to get started. If you yield to procrastination or have misplaced the materials you need to get the job done, it is easy to become discouraged before the actual work is even begun.

# FREEDOM WITHIN LIMITS: THE POETRY OF SELF-CONTROL

Poetry is a great exercise for helping develop mental self-control and fostering academic success. Because of the limiting form and function (you have to be precise in expressing what you want to say), it enhances focus and allows the writer to think outside of the box. Try this simple exercise for setting goals: 1) Think of the goal you want to achieve, such as developing better self-control by studying earlier for the next test; 2) Use a set number of lines to express this desire in a poem—say five to ten lines; 3) Revise the poem until it is as close to perfect as you can make it.

## STRATEGIES FOR SELF-CONTROL

Strategies of self-regulation in the school environment usually involve three areas: personal, behavioral, and environmental. What follows are suggestions for how to improve in each of these three categories.

## PERSONAL

Personal self-regulation involves how to organize and interpret information, whether during a lecture or when studying for a test. Begin by interacting with the information by incorporating such techniques as outlining, summarizing, highlighting key points, and using flashcard. You can also draw pictures, diagrams, or charts.

Getting organized can be as simple as using a monthly planner to keep track of upcoming tests, projects, and assignments.

Try a combination of these information-processing techniques. They are good ways to retain the necessary information longer and understand it better.

Work on time management and pacing. It helps to know which subject, project, or task should be started first and to estimate how much time will be needed to prepare. Having a separate notebook for each subject to record upcoming tests, projects, and assignments will help with this process. Even the use of a simple monthly planner is a good step toward keeping organized.

Keep the most important papers—like notices, project details, and instructions—in one place. This will save a lot of time. Even something as simple as a two-pocket folder in which one side is labeled "To Do" and the other "Done" is another effective organizational technique.

A third aspect of personal self-regulation is adequate recordkeeping and monitoring. Take notes in each class and keep them in separate binders or folders. Keep any handouts in chronological order in the specific subject notebook. They will be much quicker and easier to access this way.

## BEHAVIORAL

Behavioral strategies for developing self-control are specific actions that the student takes. These strategies can be categorized as either self-evaluating or self-consequating. With self-evaluating behaviors, the student takes responsibility for checking his or her own quality and progress. Keep the teacher in the loop and ask for suggestions on how to improve work on the assignment or project while it is still in progress. In this way, there will be time to make changes before the final due date. Take responsibility for your own self-control and attentiveness. Pay careful attention to directions and instructions. Many poor grades are given simply because the instructions were not followed correctly.

Self-consequating behavior refers to taking charge of your own motivation. This could involve arranging for rewards or punishments as a way to self-reinforce. Be in charge of your own delayed gratification strategies. Watch television after homework is finished. Reward yourself with a shopping trip only after that exam has been successfully passed.

A structured physical environment will promote effective study. Use a sturdy chair and a clean workspace that is free of noise and other distractions.

## ENVIRONMENTAL

Environmental strategies for developing self-control in the school setting involve seeking help or assistance from others and appropriately structuring your work and study environment.

Review where the best sources of information are located. The library? The Internet? Remember to go back over old tests and earlier chapters from textbooks as review. Often review tests and questions, sample key words, or important main points to remember are found at the end of each chapter. These are excellent built-in study tools.

Structuring the environment involves the physical setting that will make for effective study and that will also eliminate or minimize distractions. Avoid studying in front of the television or on a bed. A comfortable office chair and a clean workspace such as a desk or dining room table often serve as excellent study areas. It is also appropriate and advisable to plan regular, widely spaced breaks in your study time. This allows for longer stamina in study sessions and sharper thinking.

The final aspect of the environmental category is social assistance. This assistance could come from teachers, adults, other classmates, or even tutors. Success does not have to be a solitary pursuit. There are plenty of academic resources ready at hand. Join or organize a study group. Set a definite start and stop time with the group to maximize study time and set expectations.

Every student has the gift of free will and self-determination. Self-control means deliberately choosing to exercise willpower and delayed gratification. It is the ability to block out distractions, irritations, frustration, and boredom in order to achieve an end goal. By exercising self-discipline, academic success is well within reach and can begin today!

# CHAPTER 4

# PHYSICAL SELF-CONTROL

Ryan had struggled with weight issues his entire life. He had asthma, and, as a result, his doctor prescribed steroids. The steroids made him extremely hungry. And because of his asthma, he didn't go outside very much. So all he did was stay indoors and eat. By the time Ryan was in ninth grade, he weighed 310 pounds (141 kilograms). He was terribly depressed at that point. He finally took a look in the mirror and decided that he was the only one who could change things. He had to force himself to take the first step. He needed to take responsibility and start using self-control.

Ryan joined marching band to get outside and get some exercise. He started playing tennis. He took control of his diet, started eating healthier, and even found himself smiling more. Four years later, he weighs 159 pounds (72 kg), gets better grades, and is the drum major for his marching band. He is so much happier and so grateful that he decided to take control of his life.

Physical self-control involves such areas as diet, physical fitness, and the avoidance of drugs and alcohol. Individuals with good physical self-control have better mastery over their physical bodies and appetites. This means they take care of their bodies and are much less likely to abuse alcohol and drugs. They are also less likely to have unhealthy or self-destructive eating patterns like obesity or bulimia. A person with strong physical self-control will generally have more energy, experience better mood control, and enjoy better overall physical health. All of these lead to a much happier life in general.

## DIET

Not every food is created equal. Some foods have more nutrients and healthful substances than others. Good health requires knowledge and wisdom regarding not only which foods to eat but also which foods to avoid or eat sparingly. But no single food has all the nutrients a body requires to maintain good physical health. People need to eat a variety of wholesome foods from the five food groups: grains, vegetables, fruits, dairy, and protein (meat and beans). Foods that are high in fat or sugars should be eaten sparingly. Most junk foods contain a high concentration of fats and sugars. Eating a lot of junk food can lead to such health complications as obesity, tooth decay, and digestive complications. It can also create a general feeling of sluggishness.

Not every food is created equal. Try keeping healthy, crunchy snacks readily available when self-control may be in limited supply.

We live in a time in which junk food is tasty, inexpensive, readily available, and convenient. Self-control is required in such an environment. Think junk food is quicker to grab when your stomach is rumbling? Try grabbing an apple, dried fruit, or even a carrot. Keep a supply of crunchy vegetables in the refrigerator for those times when you are really hungry and self-control may be in short supply.

# PHYSICAL FITNESS

Other than running up and down the gym during PE class, many teens do not get much exercise. All teens should be physically active every day, for at least half an hour a day. This physical activity could involve taking part in community activities, family activities, school sports, individual sports, physical work (like gardening and yard work), games, and conventional workouts. There are many physical activities that a teen can pursue and enjoy. These include:

- Biking
- Jogging
- Hiking
- Tennis or volleyball
- Gymnastics
- Ice skating, rollerblades, or skateboards
- Martial arts
- Dancing
- Parkour
- Water sports
- Yoga

The list is practically unlimited! Many teens may feel discouraged if they are not naturally gifted or coordinated in a given sport or activity. But there are many activities that one can participate in, as part of a group or alone.

By being physically fit, a person is better able to enjoy school, home, and community activities. The key is just to get moving.

There may be barriers to achieving physical fitness—such as time pressures or emotional insecurity. But when you recognize what those barriers are and practice overcoming them, it eventually gets easier. The rewards of physical fitness can then be quickly realized.

When people are more physically fit, they are better able to participate in and enjoy school, family, or community activities. They have more stamina and find it easier to be a team player or participant. Trying new activities and varying workout routines can help overcome the boredom factor.

Not enough time? Once again, this is where self-control comes in. It will take commitment and willpower to get off of the couch or out of bed earlier in order to exercise or attend a team practice. Force yourself to get up and out a few times in a row and soon self-discipline won't seem so

# GO TO SLEEP!

While this area may not seem as important, getting enough sleep definitely involves a lot of self-control. It requires self-discipline to go to bed early rather than staying up late watching TV shows, texting with friends, or watching the latest YouTube videos. It may be more fun to stay up late, but getting the right amount of sleep is essential to maintaining self-control in other areas of our lives.

Sufficient sleep contributes to clear thinking, alertness, and concentration. Low-quality and insufficient sleep is attributed to poor academic performance and lower grades, as well as difficulty in controlling emotions. A sleep-deprived person is more likely to experience depression, anger problems, and fear.

So how much sleep should a teen get? The National Sleep Foundation suggests that teens get between 8.5 and 9.25 hours each and every night. Think about how grumpy, cranky, and snappy you get with people when you don't get enough sleep. It really makes a difference.

challenging. You'll be hooked on the feeling of physical health and reluctant to miss a single opportunity to exert yourself and grow even stronger and healthier.

## DRUGS AND ALCOHOL

Some people try alcohol out of curiosity or to fit in. More than 80 percent of high school students try alcohol before graduating. Digested alcohol is absorbed into the bloodstream and affects the brain and spinal cord.

Besides being illegal, drinking often makes a person look foolish and pathetic. Since it affects the nervous system, the drinker could end up doing something embarrassing. He or she might throw up, say or do things he or she will later regret, or pass out—or all three, more or less at one time. Teens who drink are also more likely to engage in dangerous or even fatal activities.

Before parties and other social gatherings, plan ahead on how to say no to drugs and alcohol and stand firm against peer pressure.

Hard to say no? Blame a parent or coach's orders when turning down a beer. Develop a game plan before a party or event that may involve drinking. Have a signal prearranged with a friend so that you both know when it's time to leave. Or plan a more stimulating and enriching activity, something other than hanging out in a basement drinking. Self-control will help you make the decision to avoid harmful temptations or peer pressure–driven social situations in advance. You can remove yourself from the situation well before the moment when you must make a split-second decision to yield to the crowd or stand firm.

Illegal drugs are illegal for a reason. They can cause great harm to you physically and emotionally. Prescription and over-the-counter drugs can be helpful or harmful depending on their purpose, dosage, and use (or mis-use). Many drugs can feel good at first but will eventually cause serious damage to both the body and brain. They can often impair one's ability to make safe, healthy, and smart choices. Drugs can ruin every aspect of a person's life. They can even erode your free will—meaning that the drug will eventually gain control of you.

The best way of dealing with drugs, alcohol, and tobacco is to never use them in the first place. It's far easier to show self-control early on by rejecting all offers of drugs and alcohol. Once you're addicted to them, your self-control will go down the drain, along with everything else that is good in your life.

# CHAPTER 5

# ACHIEVING SELF-CONTROL

Eli Flores was failing seventh grade English and getting D's in math and science. He was frustrating his teachers, and he obviously didn't want to be in school. That was before Aaron Clark began tutoring him and teaching him about self-control. Eli learned techniques for improving his study habits and grades. He would work an additional seven hours outside of the classroom each week. By the end of the year, his grades had risen from D's to mostly A's and B's. Eli received the second highest score in his district's English test. Even his penmanship and posture improved. Today, Eli is no longer frustrating his teachers or himself.

Aaron Clark knew from firsthand experience the benefits of self-control. He grew up in the same Los Angeles neighborhood as Eli. He shared the same struggles with school and living in a dangerous neighborhood. In fifth grade, Clark made a promise to himself that if he got out of the projects and made it to college, he would find a way to help kids in his own neighborhood. And he's done just that.

He learned self-control and is now teaching it to others.

Researchers have found that even the most seemingly minor exercises of self-control—like sitting up straight, eating regular and healthy meals, not biting one's nails, and keeping one's room clean—are exercises that build character strength. One study showed that people who worked daily on a single aspect of self-regulation, like the ones mentioned above, later tested better than

Even the most minor exercises of self-control, like sitting up straight and raising a hand before speaking, can provide a solid foundation for greater demonstrations of discipline that result in academic, social, and professional success and lifelong happiness.

other groups in various self-control experiments. Self-control is a muscle that gets stronger with use. So when we use and master self-control in small areas now, we become empowered to use it in other, more complex areas of our lives both now and in the future.

# WHAT'S THE BRAIN GOT TO DO WITH IT?

Self-control actually stems from not one but two regions of the brain. Our more rational long-term thoughts take place in the prefrontal cortex. This is the front part of the brain, just behind the forehead. It is also the area where good and bad choices are made, where consequences of actions are predicted, and where urges are suppressed. The prefrontal cortex comes up with the "If-Then" scenarios. This is when a person reasons, "If I obey the speed limit, not only will I not get a ticket for speeding, but I then become a safer driver."

The rational part of the brain can be trained to take charge of the self-defeating impulses of the primitive part of the brain. This is what is happening when you choose fruit over some salty and sugary processed snack.

The urgent decisions are made in the ventral striatum. The ventral striatum is also located behind the forehead but much deeper in the brain. This part of the brain is where you might think, despite being on a diet, "Gee, that candy bar sure looks good. I really, really want it. I think I'll eat it right now." Often rational thoughts from the prefrontal cortex are overruled by this more primitive part of the brain.

So is it possible for the rational part to win over the irrational, impulsive, gratification-driven primitive part? Absolutely! One obvious way is to change your focus in the environment around you. Move to a different area of the house, far away from that candy bar. Plan ahead and have healthy snacks available in the cupboard or refrigerator that can be easily grabbed. The rational part of your brain can be trained to be in charge at all times. It can be taught to overrule the negative and self-defeating impulses of the "primitive brain."

## DISTRACT YOURSELF!

The kids who were successful in delaying gratification during the marshmallow experiment used distraction to avoid temptation. For example, they covered their eyes and imagined that the treats were big puffy clouds or sang songs from *Sesame Street*. Find your own unique method of distraction for those times when temptation strikes.

# 8 STRATEGIES FOR IMPROVING SELF-CONTROL

**1)** Respect the limited resource of self-control. Recognize when self-control will be at its lowest point and plan accordingly. Temptations can be successfully avoided when you anticipate and have a plan for your weakest moments.

**2)** Make a plan for how you will avoid temptation before actually being faced with the temptation. Bring only a certain amount of money for shopping to avoid overspending. Decide exactly when and where to write that English essay to avoid procrastination. Locate the nearest trash can in the park before finishing the water bottle so that there won't be any temptation to just drop it on the ground.

**3)** Set your own rewards. Sometimes a smaller, more immediate reward helps as you are working toward the larger delayed reward. The promise of a ten-minute break after writing the first three hundred or five hundred words of that essay just may be what gets the words flowing. A series of small rewards along the way will carry you to the end of the assignment, when you can finally enjoy the movie or video game you promised yourself.

**4)** Be optimistic. People who have a positive attitude about their ability to reach a goal are more likely to achieve it.

**5)** Write it down! It has been proven that goals are easier to achieve when they are monitored. Carry a small notebook to track progress toward your goal. Journaling has been shown to have great benefits. Self-awareness is critical when monitoring your progress toward goals. Self-regulation and discipline will quickly deteriorate if focus on the behavior wanes or is lost.

**6)** Get comfortable with being uncomfortable. A little "suffering" is OK. Accept temporary failure and keep practicing. It's OK to struggle because that is where the learning and progress take place. Once a challenge or obstacle has been overcome, that moment of success can then serve as a reminder that self-control is possible and pays rich rewards.

**7)** Use self-talk. Choosing and repeating a personal mantra helps to get over those bumps in the road to self-control. "I can rise above this." "Everything is going to turn out in the end." "I'm OK." "I can do this!"

**8)** Use a role model. What would a personal hero do? Observe a respected and admired mentor and practice thinking or acting as he or she would.

# WATCH OUT! IT'S CONTAGIOUS!

The ripple effects of self-control are pretty remarkable: it can actually be contagious! We learn about the ability to control or impact the outcome of our own destiny by observing others doing the same. And, in turn, we can have the same positive effect on others.

Self-control is contagious among people and across behaviors. For example, thinking about someone else sticking to his or her diet will make an individual more likely to persist in pursuing his or her own goals, even if those goals have nothing to do with eating.

Any area that a person is able to better master through the exercise of self-control will bring short-term and long-term rewards in life. The short-term success will be that feeling of overcoming a difficult challenge or of succeeding in an area in which you have a tendency to struggle. This will bring a feeling of tremendous empowerment and self-confidence. Even if self-control is mostly being exercised in school, it can create strength when needed at home or with peers. The habitual demonstration of self-control provides a "rush" that comes from being in command and in charge of oneself. Pride and strength are among the most valuable short-term benefits of self-control.

Consistent practice of self-control in the long-term results in lifelong discipline, skill, and mastery. Any skill is more enjoyable the better one becomes at it. A person who has

Self-control can be contagious. The positive example of one person can encourage others to take control of their own destiny and make smart, healthy, and disciplined decisions that lead to success and happiness.

practiced and mastered self-control in his or her teens will become a happier and more well-adjusted adult. There is a much smaller likelihood of abusing drugs or alcohol or participating in risky behaviors. The self-controlled enjoy better mental and physical health and greater financial security. People who demonstrate self-control can more effectively manage their reactions to disappointment and insecurity. In the long run, they will be more productive in both individual and group settings, more successful, and more popular!

The person with self-control is happier, has higher self-esteem, and has better relationship skills. The family is happier. Peers are happier. Society benefits and is more harmonious. What could be better than that?

# GLOSSARY

**ANGER ENHANCER**  A physical or emotional condition that augments or heightens anger. It might be stress, fatigue, sickness, intoxication, or worry.

**BEHAVIOR**  How people act or conduct themselves.

**CALM**  Not excited or overly emotional.

**COMMUNICATE WITH RESPECT**  To talk with other people, even about difficult topics, without getting angry or making the other person feel bad.

**CONSEQUENCE**  The effect, result, or outcome of a choice or action.

**COURAGE**  The mental, emotional, or spiritual ability to face danger, fear, pain, or difficulty in order to reach a goal or act in accordance with a person's beliefs.

**DISTRACTION**  An interruption, an obstacle to concentration, or something that serves as a diversion.

**DRUG**  Any chemical substance that causes a change in a person's physical or psychological state.

**EMPOWERMENT**  The receiving of power, authority, ability, or enablement.

**ENDORPHINS**  Chemicals in the brain that are released during exercise causing excitement and happiness.

**MNEMONIC DEVICE**  Any learning technique that helps a student remember, retain, and recall information.

**MOTIVATION**  An incentive, desire to do something, or powerful reason to act in a certain way.

**REDIRECT**  To place attention somewhere else rather than on a negative thought or situation.

**RELAX** To grow calm after being upset, stressed out, or highly emotional.

**SELF-CONTROL** Restraint of one's actions, thoughts, feelings, and impulses.

**SUCCESS** A favorable outcome of something attempted.

**TOOL** A special instrument or capability that makes it easier to approach or solve a problem or to achieve a goal.

**TRIGGER** A word, action, or thought that causes an angry or other emotional response.

**WILLPOWER** The ability to exert control over one's actions, desires, and impulses.

American Psychological Association (APA)
750 First Street NE
Washington, DC 20002-4242
(800) 374-2721 or (202) 336-5500
Web site: http://www.apa.org
The APA is the largest scientific and professional psychological organization in the United States. On its Web site are links to various topics and information, including anger management.

Canadian Positive Psychology Association (CPPA)
1 Eglinton Avenue East, Suite 407
Toronto, ON M4P 3A1
Canada
(416) 481-8930
Web site: http://www.positivepsychologycanada.com
The CPPA is a not-for-profit-organization dedicated to the improvement of psychological health across Canada. Its Web site lists events, positive psychology conference information, and links to research papers about positive psychology.

CHARACTER COUNTS!/Josephson Institute of Ethics
9841 Airport Boulevard, Suite 300
Los Angeles, CA 90045
(800) 711-2670 or (310) 846-4800
Web site: http://www.charactercounts.org

This nationwide nonprofit initiative supports nonpartisan, nonsectarian character education.

Character Education Partnership (CEP)
1025 Connecticut Avenue NW, Suite 1011
Washington, DC 20036
(800) 988-8081
Web site: http://www.character.org
The CEP is a national umbrella group for numerous character education organizations. Its Web site provides resource lists, bulletin boards, and other useful information.

Developmental Studies Center (DSC)
2000 Embarcadero, Suite 305
Oakland, CA 94606
(800) 666-7270
Web site: http://www.devstu.org
The DSC is a nonprofit educational publisher dedicated to children's academic, ethical, and social development.

GoodLife Kids Foundation
201 King Street
London, ON N6A 1C9
Canada
(519) 661-0190, ext. 273

Web site: http://www.goodlifekids.com

The GoodLife Kids Foundation strives to "inspire, support, and create opportunities to help kids live more active and healthy lives." The organization offers resources on its Web site, including recipes and activities, and provides grants to other organizations that offer sustainable physical activity programs for youths.

National Crime Prevention Council (NCPC)
2001 Jefferson Davis Highway, Suite 901
Arlington, VA 22202-4801
(202) 466-6272
Web site: http://www.ncpc.org/training

The NCPC offers tools, resources, training, and programs for communities, individuals, and families to prevent crime. The site also contains links to articles on helping teens manage conflict and anger.

Positive Coaching Alliance (PCA)
Department of Athletics
Stanford University
Stanford, CA 94305-6150
(866) 725-0024
Web site: http://www.positivecoach.org

The PCA is a national nonprofit organization dedicated to providing youth with positive, character-building sports experiences. It provides tools, guidelines, and programs to help coaches develop good character in young athletes.

VIA Institute on Character
312 Walnut Street, Suite 3600
Cincinnati, OH 45202
(513) 621-7501
Web site: http://www.viacharacter.org
VIA encourages the development of character strengths that can be applied to work, family, and peer relationships and lead to great success in all aspects of one's life.

## WEB SITES

Due to the changing nature of Internet links, Rosen Publishing has developed an online list of Web sites related to the subject of this book. This site is updated regularly. Please use this link to access the list:

http://www.rosenlinks.com/7CHAR/Cont

# FOR FURTHER READING

Berry, Joy. *Winning Skills: You Can Be in Control.* New York, NY: Joy Berry Enterprises, 2010.

Biegel, Gina. *The Stress Reduction Workbook for Teens: Mindfulness Skills to Help You Deal with Stress.* Oakland, CA: Instant Help, 2010.

Brier, Norman. *Enhancing Academic Motivation: An Intervention Program for Young Adolescents.* Champaign, IL: Research Press, 2010.

Brier, Norman. *Self-Regulated Learning: Practical Interventions for Struggling Teens.* Champaign, IL: Research Press, 2010.

Caselman, Tonia, and Joshua Cantwell. *Impulse Control Activities and Worksheets for Middle School Students.* Chapin, SC: Youth Light, 2009.

Craver, Marcella Marino. *Chillax! How Ernie Learns to Chill Out, Relax, and Take Charge of His Anger.* Washington, DC: Magination Press, 2011.

Denega, Danielle. *Smart Money: How to Manage Your Cash* (Scholastic Choices). New York, NY: Children's Press, 2008.

DiConsiglio, John. *True Confessions: Real Stories About Drinking and Drugs* (Scholastic Choices). New York, NY: Children's Press, 2008.

Dijk, Sheri Van. *Don't Let Your Emotions Run Your Life for Teens: Dialectical Behavior Therapy Skills for Helping You Manage Mood Swings, Control Angry Outbursts, and Get Along with Others.* Oakland, CA: Instant Help, 2011.

Hugel, Bob. *I Did It Without Thinking: True Stories About Impulsive Decisions That Changed Lives* (Scholastic Choices). New York, NY: Children's Press, 2008.

Johnson, Avery, and Roy S. Johnson. *Aspire Higher.* New York, NY: HarperCollins, 2008.

Kenny, Karen Latchana. *Strength Training for Teen Athletes: Exercises to Take Your Game to the Next Level* (Sports Training Zone). North Mankato, MN: Capstone Press, 2012.

Lamia, Mary C. *Emotions! Making Sense of Your Feelings.* Washington, DC: Magination Press, 2012.

Lamia, Mary C. *Understanding Myself: A Kid's Guide to Intense Emotions and Strong Feelings.* Washington, DC: Magination Press, 2010.

Langlas, James. *Heart of a Warrior: 7 Ancient Secrets to a Great Life.* Minneapolis, MN: Free Spirit Publishing, 2012.

Lohmann, Raychelle Cassada. *The Anger Workbook for Teens: Activities to Help You Deal with Anger and Frustration.* Oakland, CA: Instant Help, 2009.

Schechter, Lynn R. *My Big Fat Secret: How Jenna Takes Control of Her Emotions and Eating.* Washington, DC: Magination Press, 2009.

Withers, Jennie, and Phyllis Hendrickson. *Hey, Back Off!: Tips for Stopping Teen Harassment.* Far Hills, NJ: New Horizon Press, 2011.

# BIBLIOGRAPHY

American Psychological Association. "What You Need to Know About Willpower: The Psychological Science of Self-Control." 2012. Retrieved September 2012 (http://www.apa.org/helpcenter/willpower.aspx).

Boys Town. "Teaching Self-Control to Teens." Parenting .org, 2012. Retrieved July 2012 (http://www.parenting .org/article/teaching-self-control-teens).

Cambridge Educational. "C.A.G.E. the rage: handling Your Anger." 2007. Retrieved July 2012 (http://fmghttp .iriseducation.org/169/93/36107_guide.pdf).

Character Education. "Handling Emotions." GoodCharacter .com. Retrieved July 2012 (http://www.goodcharacter .com/MStopics.html).

Conflict Resolution in Education. "Anger: A Secondary Emotion." 2012. Retrieved August 2012 (http://www .creducation.org/resources/anger_management/ anger__a_secondary_emotion.html).

Dean, Jeremy. "Top 10 Self-Control Strategies." PsyBlog, April 2011. Retrieved June 2012 (http://www.spring.org .uk/2011/04/top-10-self-control-strategies.php).

Duckworth, Angela L. "Self-Discipline Is Empowering." BACKTALK, March 2009. Retrieved June 2012 (http://www.sas.upenn.edu/~duckwort/images/self-discipline%20is%20empowering.pdf).

Duckworth, Angela L. "The Significance of Self-Control." PNAS.org, February 7, 2011. Retrieved June 2012 (http://www.pnas.org/content/108/7/2639.full).

Duckworth, Angela L., and Martin E. P. Seligman. "Self-Discipline Outdoes IQ in Predicting Academic Performance of Adolescents." *Psychological Science*, 2005. Retrieved May 2012 (http://www .sas.upenn.edu/~duckwort/images/Psychological ScienceDec2005.pdf).

Encyclopedia of Mind Disorders. "Self-Control Strategies." Retrieved September 2012 (http://www .minddisorders.com/Py-Z/Self-control-strategies .html#b%23ixzz27QuCJJy6).

Hall, K. "Knowing Your Emotions: Internal Triggers." Psych Central, 2012. Retrieved September 2012 (http://blogs .psychcentral.com/emotionally-sensitive/2012/01/ knowing-your-emotions-internal-triggers).

Harrison, Paul. "Self Master: How to Control Feelings and Emotions." ARoleModel.com, May 29, 2012. Retrieved June 2012 (http://arolemodel.com/2012/05/29/self -mastery-how-to-control-feelings-and-emotions).

Jenkins, Bill. "What Does the Marshmallow Experiment Tell Us About Self-control?" *Science of Learning*, January 24, 2012. Retrieved September 2012 (http://www.scilearn.com/blog/marshmallow -experiment-self-control-young-children.php).

Johnson, Avery, and Roy S. Johnson. *Aspire Higher.* New York, NY: HarperCollins, 2008.

Lee, Ken. "Aaron Clark Beat the Odds, Now Helps Other Kids Succeed." *People*, June 14, 2012. Retrieved

September 2012 (http://www.people.com/people/article/0,,20603351,00.html).

Lehrer, Jonah. "Don't! The Secret of Self-Control." *New Yorker*, May 18, 2009. Retrieved July 2012 (http://www.new yorker.com/reporting/2009/05/18/090518fa_fact_lehrer).

Mabuse, Nkepile. "Michaela DePrince: From War Orphan to Teen Ballerina." CNN, September 3, 2012. Retrieved August 2012 (http://www.cnn .com/2012/08/29/world/africa/michaela-deprince -ballet-dancing/index.html).

McCarron, Joshua. "Self-Control Techniques for Teenagers." LiveStrong.com, June 21, 2010. Retrieved July 2012 (http://www.livestrong.com/article/154724 -self-control-techniques-for-teenagers).

National Crime Prevention Council. "Helping Teens Manage Conflict." August 2006. Retrieved August 2012 (http:// www.ncpc.org/programs/teens-crime-and-the- community/monthly-article/helping-teens-manage -conflict).

Nauert, Rick. "Subliminal Trigger of Emotions." Psych Central News, April 29, 2008. Retrieved August 2012 (http://psychcentral.com/news/2008/04/29/subliminal -trigger-of-emotions/2200.html).

Niemiec, Ryan M. "Character Strengths and Goal-Setting." VIA Institute on Character. Retrieved September 2012 (http://viapros.org/www/en-us/resources/character strengthsandgoalsettingarticle.aspx).

Peterson, Christopher, and Martin E. P. Seligman. *Character Strengths and Virtues*. New York, NY: Oxford University Press, 2004.

Polk County Public Schools. "October's Key to Character: Self-Control." October 2007. Retrieved August 2012 (http://www.polk-fl.net/staff/resources/documents/keystocharacter/October2007.pdf).

Schute, Nancy. "For Kids, Self-Control Factors into Future Success." National Public Radio, February 14, 2011. Retrieved September 2012 (http://www.npr.org/2011/02/14/133629477/for-kids-self-control-factors-into-future-success).

Seligman, Martin E. P. *Authentic Happiness.* New York, NY: Free Press, 2003.

Siegle, Dan, and Sally Reis. "Self-Regulation." The National Research Center on the Gifted and Talented. Retrieved July 2012 (http://www.gifted.uconn.edu/siegle/selfregulation/section0.html).

Tough, Paul. "What If the Secret to Success Is Failure?" *New York Times*, September 14, 2011. Retrieved September 2012 (http://www.nytimes.com/2011/09/18/magazine/what-if-the-secret-to-success-is-failure.html?pagewanted=all).

University of Georgia. "Self-Control, and Lack of Self-Control, Is Contagious." ScienceDaily, January 18, 2010. Retrieved September 2012 (http://www.sciencedaily.com/releases/2010/01/100113172359.htm).

# INDEX

## A

alcohol, 10, 35, 39–41, 49
anger, managing, 21–23
auto-appraiser trigger, 19

## B

behavioral strategies, 29, 31
boundaries, learning to
    enforce, 12–14
brain anatomy and self-
    control, 19, 44–45

## C

C.A.G.E. method, 22–23
Clark, Aaron 42–43

## D

delaying gratification, 4,
    7–8, 26, 32, 33, 45
DePrince, Michaela, 15–16
diagrams and charts,
    29–30
diet, 4, 34, 35–36, 45, 48
discussion (as trigger), 21
distractions, 45
Douglas, Gabby, 4–6, 9
drugs, 10, 35, 41, 49

## E

eating disorders, 35
environmental strategies,
    29, 32–33
exercise, 10, 34, 35, 37–39

## I

imagination (as trigger),
    20–21

## L

Lumbo, Januario, 24–26

## M

marshmallow experiment,
    7–8, 45
memory recall, 20

## P

personal self-regulation,
    29–31
prefrontal cortex, 44
profiles (of individuals who
    exert admirable self-
    control), 4–6, 15–16,
    24–26, 34, 42–43

# R

recordkeeping, 31
reflective appraiser trigger,
　19–20
restraint, 18

# S

school
　and delaying gratification,
　　26–27
　and poetry, 29
　tips and strategies for
　　self-control at, 20,
　　27–33
self-consequating
　behavior, 31
self-control
　benefits of, 16–18
　components of, 18
　experiments and studies
　　of, 7–8
and heredity, 9–10
learning to practice,
　11–12
a quiz to test, 10
and relationships, 18
spreading it around,
　48–49
strategies for improving,
　27–33, 46–47
what it is, 4, 8–9
sleep, 21, 39
social assistance, 33
structured environment, 33

# T

thinking deliberately, 18
time management, 30
tobacco, 41
triggers, emotional, 18–21

# V

ventral striatum, 45

## ABOUT THE AUTHOR

Ramona Siddoway is a writer who has published in several countries and three continents: Africa, Europe, and North America. It took self-control for her to sit down and write this book, especially when there were times she would rather eat a lot of snacks or watch a long movie. She is the mother of four children and lives in Houston, Texas, with her husband, an adopted African cat, and a dog with very little self-control.

## PHOTO CREDITS